SLIPPED SKIN

Katie Hale is a novelist and poet, based in Cumbria. Her poetry collection, *White Ghosts*, won a Northern Debut Award, and she is the author of two novels: *The Edge of Solitude* and *My Name is Monster*. She is a former MacDowell Fellow, and winner of the Palette Poetry Prize, Munster Chapbook Prize, and Aesthetica Creative Writing Prize, and has held Writer in Residence positions in the US, Australia and Svalbard. Katie also mentors young writers through Writing Squad.

Also by Katie Hale

The Edge of Solitude	(Canongate, 2024)
White Ghosts	(Nine Arches Press, 2023)
My Name is Monster	(Canongate, 2019)
Assembly Instructions	(Southword, 2019)
Breaking the Surface	(Flipped Eye, 2017)

CONTENTS

SELKIE, I   15

SELKIE, II   23

SELKIE, III   31

SELKIE, IV   37

ACKNOWLEDGEMENTS   41

for L, always

© 2025, Katie Hale. All rights reserved. No part of this book may be reproduced, stored in a retrieval system, or transmitted in any form or by any means, whether electronic, mechanical, photocopying, recording, or otherwise, without the prior written permission of the publisher, except in the case of brief quotations used in reviews or scholarly works.

This work may not be used for text and data mining, including (without limitation) the training of artificial intelligence technologies or systems. The author and publisher expressly reserve all rights and opt out of any applicable text and data mining exceptions.

ISBN: 978-1-917617-50-5

Cover designed by Aaron Kent

Edited and Typeset by Aaron Kent

The author has asserted their right to be identified as the author of this Work in accordance with the Copyright, Designs and Patents Act 1988.

Broken Sleep Books Ltd
PO BOX 102
Llandysul
SA44 9BG

Slipped Skin

Katie Hale

Broken Sleep Books

this is a love story

all around Scotland, you will find the selkie
seal-turned-woman-turned-seal

her story varies

but always she exists in the in-between
woman of land and sea

what if queerness also
is a place of in-between

beach-flung wrack, retracting surf
an identity where ecologies meet

a shoreline I have walked my whole life

SELKIE, I

this is a love story
so the story goes

seal / she slipped off her skin
body pulled like kelp towards the light

    sand between the novelty of toes
    tickled by her smaller roundnesses
    buttocks / breasts / soft ball of belly
bore new weight

and he
        a fisherman

shut her seal-self in a loose chink of floorboard
till she tore such dazzling blood from his cheek
screeched seal-tongue already deserting her lips

                and what would a loving man do
                    he said / but bind her

shore-bound / woman-bound

bearing his land-born children
half-fisherman half-seal
the sea a whisper in their sleep

a silver-sheen of seal-skin
found one day while playing hide and seek

    which made their mother cry
one long sad note like a ship's horn

surrender herself back to the tide

My partner is teaching me to swim.

Or rather, she is helping my body to remember, guiding me back to the water. As a child, I spent whole summers at the local pool, turning somersaults, timing myself to hold my breath, diving for plastic toys on the bottom. But in the years since, I've got out of the habit. Work, sleep, and hoovering have snuck up on me, and I've let my water muscles forget – till swimming has become an unpractised language. A forgotten tongue. I'm loath to be out of my depth. I've developed a terror of getting water on my face, and the thought of putting my whole head under has me heaving fat panicked tears.

And yet – part of me still wants this. I miss that easy movement through a second element, with its lessened gravity. I miss the muscle-knowledge; I'm sure it must lie dormant in my body.

In our first lesson, my partner, L, kicks straight out across the pool. A low sun streams through smeachy windows. Outside, two teenagers sneak a quick cigarette. I walk on tiptoes, arms hugged across my chest. The chill rises up my stomach, needles in at the ribs.

I dip my face into the water – panic and gasp. Water pushes at my nostrils. It scours my mouth, rasping and abrasive. Water as a form of aggression. Water as something to be overcome. I focus so tightly on not breathing in, I forget to breathe out – so the air catches and clogs like a sob at the back of my throat. It's basic human instinct: hold onto your breath in a breathless world. Panic at lack of air.

L takes my hands and guides me across the rippling surface. Gently – gently – she breathes with me:

slowly in

                out for two

      slowly in

                      out for two

So let's start with depth. With floating.

First one foot, then the other, I unlock myself from the small blue tiles, tread water, recover old ground.

I try swimming lengths with my head on one side, so I can keep my face above the surface, dip just one ear into the water – as if that might be enough to translate its unfamiliar tongue. I swim. I listen. I try to understand. The voice of the pool is that of an organism: shifting liquid cells, cavernous heartbeat – which is, of course, only an amplification of my own. For the first time in years, I feel this whispered urge to slip my whole head under, to let the water surround me, soft as a pillow. *Go on*, the water whispers. *Come in…* My body resists.

After, my stomach is an undertow, my skin a sack of craving. I feel like I could eat for days.

SELKIE, II

this is a love story
so the story goes

woman / she slipped off her dress

kindled the eye of the god of the sea
till his gaze grew red tangle
roiled on its own rough waves

salt-skinned   burning
his teeth spat foam
that clung like wet fur to her legs

          still, he loved her
          or so his story goes

          lapped her with sweet wavelets
          clung oyster pearls at her throat
          islanded her to feel his surf's embrace

          and really what else could he do
          but give her flippers / blubber for the pressing deep
          re-skin her in his own image

cumbersome on the land she used to love

story goes she drowned in him

Around 370 million years ago, the first vertebrates are thought to have left the ocean. The weather was likely mild. The day calm and possibly windless, green with trees and ferns. From the flat warmth of the shallows, the first fish-like creatures pulled themselves up and onto the land.

These were the ancestors of the modern seal. They were also our ancestors. Seals, like us, are mammals: giving birth to live young; suckling them with milk; breathing air – not water.

Millions of years later, after our ancestral lineage had split, and we and the seals had gone our separate ways, some of the descendants of these first fish-like creatures found themselves reinhabiting the ocean – but this was not a regression, not quite a return. They were no longer the same organisms they had been before. Instead, they were forever changed by their time on the land, and they carried that change within them. No longer a species of one thing or the other, but creatures of the land-sea: sleek and streamlined in water, drawn to beaches to breed, to the surface for breath. They were one thing and another. They had become both.

People – like seals, porpoises and whales – also carry something of the surface when we swim underwater. We carry breath: carry it in our lungs or in diving bells or in SCUBA tanks strapped to our backs. We bring it with us: something of the above taken into the world of the below.

But we are also 70% water. So, when we displace the water around us, it is with our own bodies of water. Only our skin separates the two.

We are water.

                We are breath.

We are sea.

                We are land.

        We are both.

In the local pool, I splash myself at a strange angle, and water burrows into my ear canal. It nestles into the crook of it like something furred, shifts and curls, purrs against the drum. All day I carry these small drops with me: token, trophy. Breath carried into the deep, water carried back into the light.

SELKIE, III

> *truth be told*
> *it was the shore she loved*

sand

    sand

sand like selkie
land and sea
small grit of the in-between

shore
        give way to water

water
        surrender
        a short while
        to the land

        sand

recognising like for like
body of muscle and bone
                / of water

  stay

            sand

seek out small places
    tide-rippled
    wave-drawn
rub raw the second skin from my bones

sand
kelp
bladderwrack
clam shell
miniscule pearlescent spirals

flat wet pillow of a washed-up jellyfish
body all water-pulled-from-water

sand hoppers who flit   scatter
legs like pianists' fingers

                                                            linger

from the shore a cuckoo calls

    you-you you-you you-you

not one but two

    you-you

      you-you

               stay

Through the saltwater, sun mottles our skin green and gold, a cascade of foliage and coins. Below the surface, L's body is refracted. As waves rearrange the world above, as the depth flickers, lines that were once solid begin to ripple and reform, the borders of the body remaking themselves over and over. Despite this, there's a clarity to the body seen through water: a long high note, like a harp string plucked and sounding on and on into an empty room with high ceilings, filled with light. I swim down, touch her calf with an outstretched hand, and the note rings pure.

I am here. I am under the water. I am inside it.

Around us, tiny bubbles swirl and drift. A curl of gutweed sways to the pull of the tide. Limpet shells, mussel shells, a razor clam litter the furrowed sand below.

I come up. Breathe.

After, we sit in the sun, eat toast and apricot jam, enormous orange segments bursting with juice. L makes excellent strong coffee, and we drink it with an audience of sparrows, goldfinches, a cuckoo calling

you-you you-you

Sand still glittering our skin.

SELKIE, IV

woman   /   seal
as though the two were mutually exclusive

so her story goes
she slips one skin from her shoulders

another, silken underneath

you-you

you-you

yes, I want to tell her
this is a love story

yes *you*

ACKNOWLEDGEMENTS

Slipped Skin was written and photographed during a residency with An Tobar & Mull Theatre. It was part of a Developing Your Creative Practice project funded by Arts Council England.

LAY OUT YOUR UNREST